Growing Up DINO

Plateosaurus
(PLAT-ee-oh-
SOR-uhss)
and nest

by
Scott Ciencin

with
Matthew T. Carrano, Ph.D.
Consultant

Scholastic Inc.

New York   Toronto   London   Auckland   Sydney
Mexico City   New Delhi   Hong Kong   Buenos Aires

ISBN 0-439-83874-6

Designer: Lee Kaplan.

Cover illustration and title page: *Plateosaurus* and nest © H. Kyoht Luterman.

Back cover illustration: *Diplodocus* and calf © Julius Csotonyi.

All Ty the *Tyrannosaurus rex* illustrations by Ed Shems.

Interior graphic illustrations by Yancey Labat.

All 3-D conversions by Pinsharp 3D Graphics.

Interior Photo and Illustration Credits:
Page 4: *T. rex* and hatchlings © Andrew Plant.
Pages 6–7: Dinosaur nesting ground © Jorge Blanco.
Pages 8–9: *Therizinosaurus* egg © Pavel Riha.
Pages 10–11: Dino nest © H. Kyoht Luterman; *Oviraptor* © Julius Csotonyi; (blue sky) © Karl Naundorf/Shutterstock.com.
Page 12: *Orodromeus* eggs © John Bindon.
Page 13: (*Oviraptor* hatchling) © Alan Groves.
Pages 14–15: *Maiasaura* and baby © Stephen Missal; *Diplodocus* and calf © Julius Csotonyi.
Pages 16–23: All *Massospondylus* and *Allosaurus* illustrations © Stephen Missal; all *Triceratops* illustrations © Jaime Chirinos.
Page 26: (Dinosaur egg) © Sam Lee/Shutterstock.com; (world map) NASA/R.
Page 27: (Fossilized baby *Mussaurus*) © Louie Psihoyos/Corbis.
Page 28: (Dino bone histology) both photos courtesy of Kristi Curry Rogers; (dino bone with growth rings) © Allen Press, photo courtesy of Matthew Carrano.
Page 29: (*Therizinosaurus* eggs) © Louie Psihoyos/Corbis; (CT scan of dino egg) © Dr. Neil Clark, Hunterian Museum, University of Glasgow.
Page 30: (Kristi Curry Rogers) © Ray Rogers; (sandstone background) © John Philip Wall/Shutterstock.com.
Page 31: *Hypacrosaurus* and hatchlings © Stephen Missal; (blue sky) © Marilyn Barbone/Shutterstock.com.
Page 32: *Corythosaurus* defending nest © Stephen Missal.

12 11 10 9 8 7 6 5 4 3 2   6 7 8 9 10 11/0

Printed in the U.S.A.

First Scholastic printing, June 2006

TABLE OF CONTENTS

WELCOME TO

A *T. rex* feeds her hatchlings

GROWING UP DINO!

Hi again, it's me, Ty! Welcome back to another exciting trip into the world of dinos! So, how does a little guy like me get to be a great, big *T. rex*? By growing up! And that's what this whole book is about. We'll learn all sorts of stuff, like how dinos hatched from an egg, what a young dino did to survive back in the Age of Reptiles, and how scientists today learn how dinos grew. Did you know that…

Ty
Tyrannosaurus rex
(tie-RAN-oh-SOR-uhss
RECKS)

◆ Some growing dinos gained as much as 100 pounds (45 kg) a day?

◆ Some dino eggs were the size of cantaloupes?

◆ Dinos weren't born with big horns and crests?

And we'll answer questions like:

◆ How long did it take for a dino egg to hatch?

◆ Did dino moms take care of their dino babies?

◆ How did dinos grow so big?

Don't forget—when you see this symbol, put on your **3-D glasses** to see the dinos grow right before your eyes!

Ready to grow up dino? Follow the dino tracks to the next page, and let's get started!

A DINO'S GUIDE TO

If you took a trip back in time to when dinos were alive, the dinos that you'd probably see wouldn't be as big as the skeletons in museums. Most of the dinos that you'd spot would be small and still growing up, just like Ty!

I've still got a few tons to go!

In this book, you'll read everything you need to know about how dinos grew up. First, you'll get to peek inside a real egg in **Eggs-cellent Eggs**. Then, you'll see how dino parents took care of their babies, from hatching eggs to raising young dinos (if they did any babysitting at all!) in **Meet the Parents**.

A dinosaur
nesting ground

GROWING UP

Then you'll follow three dinos
as they go from tiny dino-tots to some of
the biggest animals that ever walked the earth in
From Hatchling to Humongous. And make sure
to check out **How Do We Know How Dinos Grew?**
to see what scientists are digging up on growing dinos all
around the world.

Ready to *grow*? Turn the page and let's get started!

EGGS-CELLENT EGGS

While dinos were some of the biggest animals ever, they weren't born that way! They all started life as tiny dinos inside an egg.

While an egg might look small on the inside, it had everything it needed for a growing dino baby. Check out this *Therizinosaurus* (THER-uh-ZEEN-oh-SOR-uhss) egg for more info!

The **embryo** (EM-bree-oh) is the dino baby that grows inside an egg before it hatches.

The **yolk** gives the growing embryo plenty of food inside the egg.

Dinosaurs laid eggs that were hard-shelled, like birds' eggs. This hard **eggshell** protected the embryo and everything else inside.

The **albumen** (AL-byoo-men) is a clear jelly that protects the embryo from getting bumped around while it's in the egg.

Eggshell walls had tiny holes called **pores** that let gases in and out to let the embryo breathe. Pores also let a little bit of water in and out of the egg, too.

DINO DATA

The first dino eggs were found in France in the late 1800s. The eggs belonged to *Hypselosaurus* (hip-SELL-oh-SOR-uhss), a long-necked, plant-eating dino. But these dino eggs were empty! The first eggs with dino babies inside weren't found until the late 1970s, in the nests of the duck-billed dino *Maiasaura* (MY-uh-SOR-uh) from Montana.

Funny Bones

Q: Why can't you tell a dino egg a joke?

A: Because it *cracks* up!

Looks like it's a tight squeeze!

MEET THE PARENTS

Just like you, dinos had a mom and dad, too. While dino parents weren't much like your mom and pop, they took enough care of their babies to help them survive. Read on to find out what dino parents did for their growing dino babies.

A dino nest

Nifty Nests

Just like most modern-day reptiles and birds, dinos made nests for their eggs. But unlike most birds, dinos made their nests on the ground. No climbing trees for dinos! When the dino mom was ready to lay eggs, she used her hands and feet to dig a shallow bowl. The bowl kept the eggs together and stopped them from rolling away.

Two By Two

Scientists think that most dino moms laid two eggs at a time, since fossilized dino nests show that the eggs are paired up.

The pairs of eggs are usually in a circle around the edge of the nest. Scientists think that dino moms stood outside the nest and turned after they laid each pair of eggs to make this circle. This might have helped the dino not step on eggs she'd already laid.

DINO DATA

A long-necked, plant-eating dino called a **sauropod** (SAW-roh-pod) might have laid up to 500 eggs over 40 years.

Warm and Toasty

Eggs need to be **incubated** (IN-cue-bay-ted) or kept warm. Without heat, embryos wouldn't grow into healthy baby dinos. Too much heat could kill embryos, too, so dino parents had to get it just right.

Dino Dictionary

To *incubate* an egg is to heat it so that it stays at the right temperature for hatching.

Sitting Pretty

Smaller dinosaurs, like **Oviraptor** (OH-vih-RAP-tore), might have sat on their eggs to keep them warm, just like birds do. Dinos who sat on their eggs might have spent part of their time sitting on the eggs and the rest away from the nest looking for food. Or, they might've eaten a lot before they laid eggs and didn't leave the nest at all.

No Scrambled Eggs

Some dinos were way too big to sit on their nests. If they did, they might have scrambled the eggs! So how did these dinos incubate their eggs? Really BIG mommas probably covered their eggs with dead leaves and plants. The rotting plants gave off heat to keep the eggs warm, and they kept the hot sun from frying the eggs, too.

Oviraptor sitting on its nest

Orodromeus
(OR-oh-DROM-ee-uhss)
eggs

Ready or Not, Here I Come!

Now it's time for what we've all been waiting for. It's time for these dino eggs to hatch! What was it like for dino babies to break out of their eggshells? Read on and find out!

Getting Warmer

No one knows for sure how long dino babies hung out in the egg, but scientists can look at modern-day animals for clues. Crocodiles take about 64–70 days of incubation to hatch, but hatching times can be very different. A spiny soft-shelled turtle only needs a month to hatch, but some tortoises can take over a year! How warm an egg is kept during incubation can speed up hatching time, too. Just 7° F (4° C) hotter can cause a desert iguana to hatch 27 days early!

Cracking Up

So how did an embryo know it was time to bust out? Some scientists think that baby dinos knew it was time to lose the eggshell when they got too big or ran out of food inside the egg. Birds and crocs have an *egg tooth* or a ridge on their beaks and snouts that help them crack egg walls, but scientists don't think that dinos had egg teeth to help them out. Baby dinos probably used their strong legs to kick against the eggshell to make their escape.

DINO DATA

Croc and bird babies croak or chirp just before they hatch from their eggs. This lets their parents know it's time to dig the eggs out if they've covered them up with leaves or it's time to stop sitting on that nest! Although scientists have no way of knowing, dino babies might have made noise to let the 'rents know that it was time to hatch, too.

Oviraptor hatchling

Dino Parenting 101

So, what did dino parents do after those eggs hatched? Since dinos aren't alive today, paleontologists aren't really sure. Check out these pages for three ways dinos might have raised their babies.

I Want My Mommy!

Some dinos probably stayed around the nest and took care of their babies for a little while, from a few weeks to a couple of months. During this time, a dino mom probably brought her hatchlings food and protected them from danger, like hungry predators.

Maiasaura
and baby

Home Alone

Scientists think that some dino parents didn't do much looking out for their kids. Some dinos probably guarded the nest until the babies hatched, and then they took off—leaving the hatchlings to look after themselves. Some dino moms probably didn't even hang around that long. They just laid their eggs and left!

So how was a newborn baby dino supposed to survive all by itself? Well, baby dinos weren't totally defenseless. By looking at fossilized dino eggs and embryos, scientists have found that some dino babies were born with strong teeth and legs, which meant they could eat on their own and run away from predators.

Family Time

Some dino parents might have taken care of their young longer than a few months…maybe even years! Like some animals alive today, it's possible that some dino babies stayed with their families all their lives, traveling in large groups called **herds**. But scientists who study dino herd tracks aren't sure if this is true. The smallest footprints are only half the size of the adults, which probably means that some young dinos didn't travel with a herd until they were older and bigger.

DINO DATA

Scientists used to think that dinos didn't care for their babies at all until a paleontologist named Jack Horner studied the nests of a duck-billed dino named *Maiasaura*. Horner noticed that the eggshells in *Maiasaura* nests weren't just cracked open—they were completely crushed to bits. He guessed that the eggshells got this way because *Maiasaura* babies stayed in the nest for some time and walked all over them. If *Maiasaura* babies were staying near their nests, a dino mom was probably looking out for them, too.

Diplodocus
(dih-PLOD-oh-kuhss)
and calf

Now that you've learned all about how baby dinos were born and how their parents might have taken care of them, it's time to discover what happened to dino babies once they really started to grow. Read on as we follow three dinos as they go from hatchling to HUGE!

Hatching Big Plans

Compared to the size of their parents, dino babies were tiny! A long-necked, plant-eating dino as long as two school buses might hatch from an egg the size of a football. So what did that mean for a baby dino? It meant that it had some catching up to do!

Not Mini-Me

You might think that just-hatched dino babies looked like tiny adults, but that wasn't true.

Nope!
We were
way cuter!

Besides being cuter, newborn baby dinos didn't have crests or horns that adult dinos had to help them tell one another apart. Sometimes dinos didn't look much like what they'd grow up to be. Check out the hatchlings on these pages and see!

MASSOSPONDYLUS (MASS-oh-SPON-dill-uhss) was a plant-eater that lived in the Early Jurassic, 205 million years ago. *Massospondylus* was a **prosauropod** (pro-SAW-roh-pod), part of a group of long-necked plant-eaters that sometimes walked on two legs. This little *Massospondylus* grew to be 8 feet (2 m) tall and walked on two legs. But at hatching, this dino baby was only 11 inches (28 cm) long, and walked on all fours.

HUMONGOUS

ALLOSAURUS
(AL-oh-SOR-uhss) was a fierce, meat-eating dinosaur that lived in the Late Jurassic, 145 million years ago. It's hard to believe, but this cute little dino grew into a giant adult 10 feet (3 m) tall and 39 feet (12 m) long. But when this baby *Allosaurus* hatched, it was only 15 inches (38 cm) long!

TRICERATOPS (try-SER-uh-TOPS) was a **ceratopsian** (SER-uh-TOP-see-un)
that lived during the Late Cretaceous, 67 million years ago. When it hatched, this dino didn't look much like an adult—it only had a small flap on its head for a frill and had no horns at all! A full-grown *Triceratops* was about 6 feet (2 m) high and 26 feet (8 m) long, but a *Triceratops* fresh from the egg was only 15 inches (38 cm) long!

Dino-Tots

For the first five years after breaking out of the egg, dino hatchlings grew nonstop. A dino like *T. rex* probably gained one pound (½ kg) every single day. While that might not seem like a lot, at the end of five years, a *T. rex* weighed 1–2 *tons*! What else did these dino-tots do?

Gettin' the Grub

Young dinos needed lots of grub in order to feed their fast-growing bodies. How did they get their claws on the good stuff? Young meat-eating dinos probably looked for prey that was small, like lizards and slow-moving insects. They might have also **scavenged** (SCAV-enjed) by eating the leftovers of bigger hunters.

Dino Dictionary

When an animal *scavenges*, it eats animals that are already dead or were killed by another animal.

Plant-eating dinos also had to learn how to find food. Did Mom and Pop show Junior the best places to find tasty greens? Nobody knows, but even if they had to figure it out by themselves, these hungry tots probably picked it up pretty fast.

MASSOSPONDYLUS

Compared to the hatchling on page 16, you can see that this dino-tot is starting to grow a longer head, neck, and body. Scientists aren't quite sure when *Massospondylus* made the change from walking on all fours to two feet, but as a dino-tot, *Massospondylus* was about 20 percent of its full-grown size, making it 4 feet (1 m) long.

Hiding Out

The first five years were really tough for a baby dino! The Mesozoic wasn't a safe place for a young tot still learning the ropes. It was an easy target for a hungry predator looking for a quick snack! Like other baby animals today, young dinos were probably experts at hiding behind rocks and plants and staying very still to blend into their surroundings.

ALLOSAURUS

After five years, little Al here has packed on the pounds, weighing in at 400 pounds (181 kg) and was about 10 feet (3 m) long. Scientists think that Al would have been about 25 percent of its full-grown size at this point.

TRICERATOPS

Scientists don't have many fossils showing how fast *Triceratops* hatchlings grew. They guess that *Triceratops* grew to about a quarter of its adult size, making it about 5 feet (1½ m) long after five years.

Not So Little Now

After the first ten years, a young dino wasn't so small anymore! The next stage in life, called **adolescence** (ad-uh-LESS-uhns), also meant big changes for these dinos. And we mean BIG! During the next few years of their lives, dinosaurs went through a **growth spurt** where they grew even faster!

Dino Dictionary

The period of time before an animal becomes an adult is called *adolescence*. A *growth spurt* is the time during adolescence where an animal does most of its growing.

MASSOSPONDYLUS

After ten years, *Massospondylus* walked on two feet. Scientists think that standing helped *Massospondylus* reach more leaves and plants and helped it run faster, as well.

Growing, Growing, Gone!

By adolescence, a dino like *T. rex* grew super-fast. Scientists guess that this dino gained about 4½ pounds (2 kg) a day until it reached full size, around 6 tons. That's three times as much as it grew in the first ten years of its life!

For sauropods, these dinos might have gained four times as much weight once they finished their growth spurt. Scientists guess that *Argentinosaurus* (are-jen-TEEN-oh-SOR-uhss), the largest known dino today, put on 100 pounds (45 kg) a day during its growth spurt.

ALLOSAURUS

At 13 feet (4 m) long, the adolescent *Allosaurus* was probably big enough to hunt larger prey. But Al still had some growing to do!

TRICERATOPS

At 20 feet (6 m) long, *Triceratops* was almost full-grown. Turn the page and see this dino all grown up!

All Grown Up

It seems like it was only yesterday that our three dinos were hatchlings that had just busted out of the egg. Doesn't time fly?

Or maybe it was only a few pages ago!

Once their growth spurt was finished, dinos were officially adults. But dinos weren't done with growing just yet! Read on to find out why!

Showing Off

Scientists know that at the end of adolescence, a dino's crests and horns grew to full size. A dino's crests and horns were important because they helped the dino to defend itself from enemies and to attract a mate so that it could have babies of its own.

Sky's the Limit

Unlike humans, dinos never stopped growing! Once dinos became adults, they didn't grow as fast as they did in adolescence. Instead, they grew very slowly. As long as a dino was alive, it grew a little bit each year. That meant that the longer a dino lived, the bigger it got. Being big was a good idea for a dino—nobody bothers you much if you're way bigger than them!

MASSOSPONDYLUS

Would you have ever guessed that this adult *Massospondylus* grew from the tiny hatchling you saw on page 16? Probably not! At 16 feet (5 m) long, this *Massospondylus*'s long neck let it reach high branches for tons of tasty greens! Since this dino didn't use its hands to walk anymore, it probably used them to tear away tough roots and vines to reach food lower to the ground.

ALLOSAURUS

Our pal Al reached full size at 39 feet (12 m) long and was one of the fiercest predators of the Jurassic. Check out the crests above Al's eyes. They probably helped other *Allosaurus* know that Al was one of their kind, too.

TRICERATOPS

At the end of adolescence, *Triceratops*'s horns grew to full size. At 29½ feet (9 m) long and as heavy as an elephant, this dino could've given an enemy a sharp poke to let it know who was boss!

HOW DO YOU MEASURE

While it's true that you'll never be as big as a *Triceratops*, you and a growing dino have more in common than you might think! These two pages compare how humans (like you!) grow compared to one of our favorite dinos, a *T. rex*.

Did someone say *T. rex*?

Baby

At birth, the average human baby weighs about 7½ pounds (3 kg) and is 19–21 inches (48–53 cm) long. In its first year, a baby grows about 10 inches (25 cm) more and triples its weight.

Upon hatching, a *T. rex* was probably only about 15 inches (38 cm) long—smaller than a newborn human when it's born!

Child

From age 2, kids only grow about 2½ inches (6 cm) a year until they reach adolescence.

For the first ten years, a *T. rex* put on 1 pound (½ kg) per day, reaching 1–2 tons by adolescence and was 25 feet (8 m) long.

Adolescent

Once humans begin adolescence (from ages 8–13 in girls and around age 15 in boys), they hit a growth spurt where they grow quickly in a short amount of time.

From ages 11–14, a *T. rex* hit its own growth spurt, gaining 4½ pounds (2 kg) a day until it reached about 3–5 tons and was almost 40 feet (12 m) long.

Adult

Once a person finished his or her growth spurt, he or she was an adult. Unlike dinosaurs and modern-day reptiles, people stop growing once they become adults.

After a *T. rex* completed its growth spurt, it kept growing slowly for the rest of its life.

HOW DO WE KNOW

Everything that scientists know about how dinos grew is from fossils. From finding fossilized dino nests and eggs to studying bits of dino bones, paleontologists have been able to put together clues to get a good picture of what it was like growing up back in the Mesozoic. Read on to learn more!

Making Ancient Eggs

A dinosaur egg

So how did dino eggs and nests become fossils? Floods, sandstorms, or erupting volcanoes quickly covered eggs and nests with mud or sand, which was the first step in becoming a fossil. And if things were just right, water soaked through eggshells and brought minerals that would let dino embryos fossilize. But that didn't happen very often!

Egg Country

Scientists have uncovered sites with thousands of dino nests grouped together. Since they've found many layers of nests and broken eggs on top of one another, scientists think that dino herds came to these spots every year to lay their eggs and raise their young.

Check out the map below to see where scientists are digging up eggs all over the world!

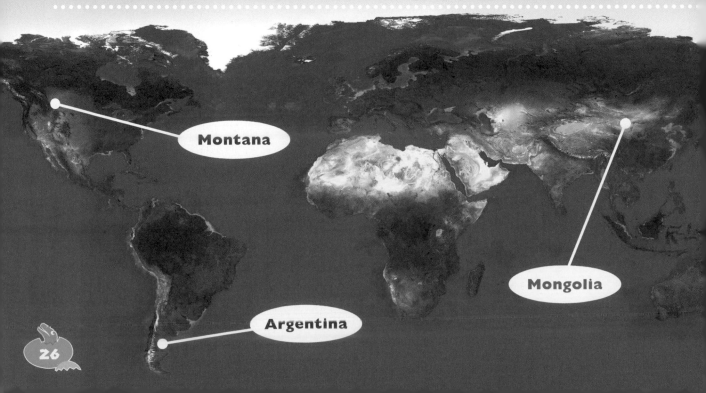

Montana

Mongolia

Argentina

HOW DINOS GREW?

All Shapes and Sizes

For many eggs, scientists don't know what kind of dino laid them since there weren't any embryos inside. But check out the chart below for some common shapes and what dinos they came from.

EGG SHAPE	SIZE	DINO
Pill-shaped	5–21 inches (13–53 cm) long, depending on the dino.	Usually belonged to meat-eating dinos called **theropods** (THAYR-oh-pods).
Round	Ranged from 5–12 inches (13–30 cm) long.	Usually belonged to long-necked sauropods.
Elliptical (one end is pointed)	About 5–8 inches (12–20 cm) long.	Horned dinos, called ceratopsians, usually laid these kinds of eggs.
Round or oval	Ranged from 3–10 inches (8–25 cm) wide.	Duck-billed dinos, like *Hypacrosaurus*, laid round or oval eggs.

Montana

Many nests have been found here, including those of **Maiasaura** and **Orodromeus**. Nests with eggs with 2-foot (½-m) long embryos of **Hypacrosaurus** (hip-PACK-kroh-SOR-uhss) were found here, too.

Argentina

In 1978, fossilized baby **Mussaurus** (moo-SOR-uhss) skeletons were found here. One of the skeletons was so small that it fit in the palm of a person's hand!

Mongolia

Baby **Bagaceratops** (BAG-uh-SER-uh-tops) have been found here, along with their nests, and **Protoceratops** (pro-toe-SER-uh-tops) and **Oviraptor** eggs and nests have been found here, too.

Fossilized baby
Mussaurus

Growth Rings: No Bones About It

One growth ring

A picture of a meat-eating dinosaur bone.
The line shows one growth ring.

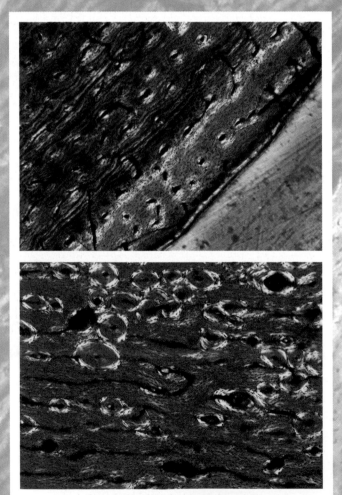

Close-up pictures of a dinosaur bone
under a special microscope.

One way that scientists study how dinos grew is by looking at **growth rings** in fossil bones. When a dino was alive and still growing, its skeleton would cover itself with a new layer of bone every year. These new layers formed rings outside the dino bones, just like the rings inside a tree's trunk.

Paleontologists who study bone **histology** (hist-TALL-loh-gee) slice fossil bones very thin and look at them under a microscope. Scientists can tell how old a dino was before it died, and they can even guess how much a dino grew in one year by measuring the thickness of one growth ring.

DINO DATA

Scientists used to think that dinosaurs grew slowly and lived for hundreds of years to get so big, like some tortoises do today. But scientists now know from studying dino bones closely that dinos grew quickly for a few years and probably only lived to be about 30–50 years old. Growth spurts (see page 20) helped dinos get big quickly so they could defend themselves better against larger predators.

Getting High-Tech

A hundred years ago, scientists probably wished they had x-ray vision to look inside a fossil egg. Today's paleontologists can do just that—and without super-powers! Nowadays scientists can use **x-ray machines** and **CT scans** to get a peek inside fossils without having to crack them open. This keeps scientists from destroying delicate egg fossils and saves lots of time and energy that's needed to study them the old-fashioned way.

A CT scan of an 80-million-year-old dino egg

X-RAY VISION

How do x-ray machines and CT scans work? Doctors use x-ray machines to shoot invisible rays that travel through clothing and skin in order to take a photograph of a person's bones. These invisible rays can also travel through the layers of rock around a fossil and let scientists study the bones inside. CT scans use x-rays, too. A computer takes many x-rays of the fossil from different angles and then puts the photographs together to make a 3-D image of the bones inside.

29

PALEONTOLOGIST

KRISTI CURRY ROGERS

Say hello to Dr. Kristi Curry Rogers, curator of paleontology at the Science Museum of Minnesota. Dr. Curry Rogers studies the way dinos grew back in the Age of Reptiles by using bone histology (see page 28). Read on to learn more about how scientists study dino growth.

Q How did you get interested in paleontology?

A When I was six or seven, I already knew that I wanted to be a paleontologist. I still have the first dinosaur thing that got my attention. It was an article on dinosaur eggs and babies found at Egg Mountain, in Montana. After I read that, it was dinos all the way!

Q When did you start studying dino bone histology?

A In college, I learned that bone histology was a way to study growth in extinct animals. I was really lucky to be at Montana State University, which had one of the only dino bone histology labs in the U.S. and I did a research project on the histology of sauropods before I graduated.

Q What's the most surprising thing you've learned about dino growth?

A I think the most surprising thing that I've learned so far about dinosaur growth is how different it was in different dinos. Really big dinos grew as fast as modern whales, and really small ones grew much slower. Even so, all dinosaurs grew at least twice as fast as any reptile alive today. But none of them grew as quickly as some kinds of birds.

Q How do you get information on growth by looking at dino bones?

A We study dinosaur bones under a microscope and look at how hard parts of a bone formed as an animal grew and for holes to see where the blood vessels were. We also look for special lines that tell us how old a dino bone is. Once we study all these things, we use math to determine how much weight a dino gained every day during its fastest time of growth.

Q Why is it important to learn how dinosaurs grew?

A Learning about dino growth helps us understand more about dinos, like how they had babies, how much food they needed, and whether or not they were warm-blooded or cold-blooded. It's also important when we look at living dinosaurs—birds. By looking at how meat-eating dinos grew, we can figure out why birds (which evolved from meat-eating dinos) grow so fast.

Dr. Curry Rogers in the field with her daughter, Lucy.

HYPACROSAURUS

Discovered in 1910 in the rocks of northern Montana, *Hypacrosaurus* (hip-PACK-kroh-SOR-uhss) was a duck-billed dino that lived 72 million years ago in the Late Cretaceous. *Hypacrosaurus* means "high-ridged lizard" which points to the crest on the top of this dino's head. This crest probably helped *Hypacrosaurus* find a mate or let other dinos know that it was a *Hypacrosaurus*.

Scientists think *Hypacrosaurus* is special because of what it left behind. A nest of eight fossilized *Hypacrosaurus* eggs with embryos was found in Devil's Coulee, near Alberta, Canada. These eggs were BIG. Each one was the size of a cantaloupe! While scientists find lots of dino eggs, they don't find eggs with embryos very often. These eggs helped them learn more about how dinos grew up back in the Mesozoic.

That's one
big omelet!

***Hypacrosaurus*
with hatchlings**

MORE DINO ADVENTURES COMING SOON!

We've come to the end of our tracks and it's been a fantastic journey! We've peeked inside a dino egg, followed young dinos as they grew to be giants, and checked out how scientists unlock secrets from dino bones. But it's not all over yet. There's plenty more to discover in the wild world of dinos! See you soon for more travels back in time!

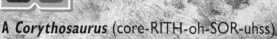

A *Corythosaurus* (core-RITH-oh-SOR-uhss) defends its nest against predators.